ICE AGE ANIMALS

RUPERT MATTHEWS

Artist: Colin Newman

The Bookwright Press
New York · 1990

Titles in this series

How Life Began
The Dinosaur Age
The Age of Mammals

Ice Age Animals
The First People
The First Settlements

Cover illustration: Mammoths and woolly rhinoceroses were two Ice Age animals.

First published in the United States in 1990 by
The Bookwright Press
387 Park Avenue South
New York NY 10016

First published in 1989 by
Wayland (Publishers) Ltd
61 Western Road, Hove
East Sussex BN3 1JD, England

Library of Congress Cataloging-in-Publication Data
Matthews, Rupert.
    Ice age animals/by Rupert O. Matthews.
      p. cm. – (Prehistoric life).
    Bibliography: p.
    Includes Index.
    Summary: Describes the great Ice Age
of the Pleistocene and its effects on the
climate, vegetation, animal life, and the
world in general.
    ISBN 0-531-18300-9
    1. Mammals, Fossils – Juvenile literature.
2. Glacial epoch-Juvenile literature.
(1. Glacial epoch. 2. Mammals, Fossil.)
I. Title.   II. Series: Matthews, Rupert. Prehistoric Life.
QE881.M44 1990
569–dc19   89–30632
                           CIP
                           AC

Typeset by Direct Image Photosetting Limited, Hove, Sussex, England.
Printed by G. Canale and C.S.p.A., Turin, Italy.

Contents

Words printed in **bold** are explained in the glossary.

The Coming of the Ice Age

About 1.5 million years ago the **climate** of the world became much colder. Winters became longer and summers shorter as temperatures fell. The Ice Age had begun.

Scientists are still not certain what caused this change in climate. The temperature of the world had been falling for several million years before the Ice Age. During this time the continents had been slowly moving as the plates of the earth's crust shifted (as they still do today).

A few million years ago, the present layout of the continents came into being. Both the North Pole and the South Pole are surrounded by land, preventing ocean currents from replacing the cold water there with warm water from the **Equator**. This allows temperatures to fall very low. It may be that the Ice Age was partly caused when the continents reached these positions.

Below **During the Ice Ages, tundra extended much farther south than it does today.**

Woolly mammoth

Woolly rhinoceros

4

A Glacier Valley

Most glaciers that formed during the Ice Age melted several thousand years ago. However, they left marks on the surface of the earth that can still be seen. Valleys that once contained glaciers are U-shaped. This was caused by the ice which carved a deep, flat-bottomed channel for itself.

As temperatures fell, winter snows near the poles and in mountains did not melt during the summer. They stayed on the ground until covered by more snow the following winter. In time the layers of snow built up to be very deep and formed ice sheets and glaciers. Glaciers are slow moving rivers of ice which gradually slide downhill to lower or warmer areas where they melt. It was these huge masses of ice, spreading out from the north and covering nearly one third of the world, that caused temperatures to drop elsewhere.

Purple areas show spread of glaciers during the Ice Age.

Changing Habitats

The biting cold and low temperatures of the Ice Age had a dramatic effect on the **environment**. The plants and the places where they grew in the world changed drastically. These changes were most noticeable in Europe, Asia and North America, where fertile land lay closest to the North Pole.

Before the Ice Age most of these lands had a warm climate, similar to that of Italy or Spain today. Trees and grass covered the land. Only very close to the North Pole was

Spring gentian

Left **As the tundra spread southward, plants such as these became more common in northern lands.**

Below **During the short summer many different plants grow on the tundra.**

Vegetation areas of the world today.

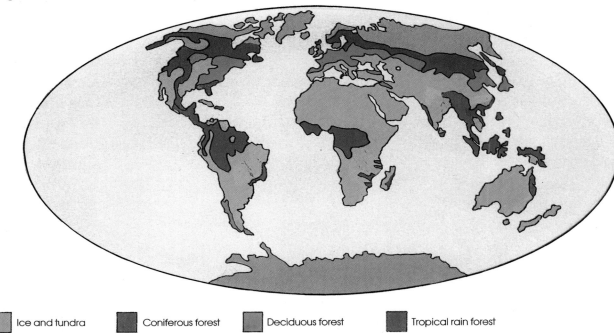

Ice and tundra | Coniferous forest | Deciduous forest | Tropical rain forest

tundra to be found.

When the Ice Age began, the spreading ice sheets pushed southward as far as central Europe. The belt of tundra that borders the ice also shifted south. At the same time it became wider, covering vast areas of land. South of the tundra was a broad zone of dense **coniferous** forest. The original **vegetation** of lush forest was only to be found close to the Equator.

This new pattern of vegetation existed for hundreds of thousands of years. It forced animals either to **migrate** southward or to **adapt** to the cold.

Left A photograph of typical coniferous forest.

On the Tundra

The weather of the tundra is extremely severe. For most of the year thick snow and freezing temperatures ensure that little survives. However during the few weeks of summer, temperatures rise to as high as 30 degrees Celsius (86°F). The snow melts and a rich carpet of grasses and other plants quickly grows and covers the ground. Thousands of insects come out of winter **hibernation** and large flocks of birds fly into the region. This burst of life is short lived. The icy cold and snow of winter soon returns.

Many animals lived on the tundra in the Ice Age. The woolly rhinoceros was very well adapted to life in a cold climate. To protect

During the Ice Ages, many animals moved onto the tundra to feed on the lush plants that grew during the summer.

Woolly rhinoceros

itself against the cold, the woolly
rhinoceros had a thick furry coat.
This coat was in two layers. Closest
to the skin grew soft, black fur
which kept the animal warm.
Reddish hairs covered the black
fur, keeping out the wind and snow.

During the short tundra summer
the woolly rhinoceros probably ate
huge amounts of grass and herbs.
This was converted into fat which
helped it to survive through the
winter when food was scarce.

Musk-ox

Dragonfly

Wolves and cave lions also lived on the tundra. The cave lion was larger than a modern lion. It probably had no mane but was covered with thick fur to protect it against the cold. It is believed that this powerful animal hunted alone. Ice Age wolves, on the other hand, were smaller animals but they hunted in packs. This made them more efficient hunters, able to deal with larger and stronger **prey** than the cave lion.

The giant deer, or Irish elk, was a huge animal, larger than any deer alive today. It stood over 2 m (6.5 ft) at the shoulder. Its antlers spread 3.7 m (12 ft) from tip to tip and may have weighed some 70 kilograms (150 lb).

Below The cave lion was a large and powerful hunter, but it is now extinct.

Cave lion

Irish elk

Wolves

Above The Irish Elk was hunted by wolves and by the cave lion. Its antlers were the largest of any deer that has ever lived.

The Tundra Today

The tundra today is far smaller than it was and several Ice Age tundra animals have died out. Irish elks, woolly rhinoceros and cave lions have all vanished. However, several other **species** remain. Huge herds of reindeer migrate to the tundra each summer as they did during the Ice Age. These herds are still followed by packs of wolves. Living all year on the tundra are musk-oxen. These strange, shaggy animals can live in

the extreme cold because they have very thick fur and they can find food even beneath deep snow.

In Northern Forests

Bordering the open tundra were huge forests of conifers and other plants able to tolerate the cold winters. The most common trees were pines and firs. Some birch, willow and hazel grew in places.

These forests were warmer than the tundra and provided shelter from cold winds. For this reason many tundra animals migrated to the forests during the winter. The **taiga** forests, as they are known, are not rich in food. In order to survive, these animals needed to store up large amounts of fat during the warm season.

Above **Reindeer were Ice Age animals.**
Below **The taiga forest sheltered many animals.**

12

Woolly mammoth

Woolly rhinoceros, reindeer and wolves all moved into the forests for the winter. But the largest of the migratory animals was the woolly **mammoth**, which was about 3.5 m (11 ft) tall. The mammoth was one of many types of elephant alive at the time. It was an unusual elephant because it was specially adapted to life in a cold climate. Its entire body was covered with thick, red-brown hair about 80 centimeters (30 in) long which kept it warm.

13

Some animals, such as the cave bear, lived in the forests throughout the year. The cave bear is so called because many skeletons have been found in caves. This does not mean that the bear lived in caves. In fact it led a life much like that of modern bears. During the summer it fed on the abundant food of the forest, storing fat under its skin. When winter came the bear would hibernate in a cave. In the spring it woke and came out to feed again.

The cave bear was huge — larger than any bear alive today. It was 3 m (10 ft) long and weighed over 700 kilograms (1,500 lb). It had strong teeth and sharp talons and would have been able to fight any other animal in the forests.

Below Possibly the largest bear ever to have lived, the cave bear is now extinct.

Cave bear

14

Wild boar

Above The wild boar was a common animal in Ice Age forests.

However, the cave bear probably ate grass and berries more than anything else.

Another fierce plant-eater of northern forests was the wild boar, which still lives in some areas. The boar stands about one meter (3 ft) high and weighs nearly 170 kilograms (375 lb) It spends most of its time eating nuts and roots. However, if it is disturbed the boar charges at high speed. The large tusks are very sharp and can kill a large animal.

Ice Age Giants

Elasmotherium

**If it was
attacked
Elasmotherium
(above) charged,
using its long
horn as a
weapon.**

The many changes of climate and vegetation during the Ice Age created great problems for animals. Some species coped with these difficulties by becoming larger. An increase in size brought several advantages. It meant that there was a smaller proportion of skin to weight. This made it easier for the animal to keep warm.

Such an advantage might explain the giants of the tundra and taiga,

but several kinds of giant animals developed far from the glaciers. These may have **evolved** because a larger individual is better able to survive attack.

In America a giant species of bison evolved which had horns measuring 2 m (6.5 ft) from tip to tip. A huge rhinoceros, known as *Elasmotherium* lived in parts of Europe and Asia. This beast was at least twice as big as a modern

16

Gigantopithecus

rhinoceros. Even more amazing was the horn, 2 m (6.5 ft) long, which grew from its skull. This animal lived on open grasslands.

Also living in Asia, and the last of its kind, was a massive ape called *Gigantopithecus*. This animal could have stood about 3 m (10 ft) tall, though it rarely raised itself on its hind feet. This makes it at least half again as large as the biggest modern gorilla.

Despite its huge size, Gigantopithecus (left) was probably a shy animal that fed on leaves and fruits.

Ice Age Pygmies

While some creatures responded to the changes of the Ice Age by increasing in size, others became smaller. This may have been due to a shortage of food. The cooling of the climate meant that there was less vegetation for plant-eaters to feed on. Under such conditions smaller animals had an advantage.

This process can be traced in the remains of the woolly mammoth. During periods of warm weather, when there was plenty of food, the mammoths increased in size. Some reached a height of 4.3 m (14 ft). When the glaciers returned and the temperatures dropped, smaller mammoths became more common, resulting in an average height of 2.75 m (9 ft).

Below Palaeoloxodon was one of several types of animals that produced miniature species during the Ice Ages.

Palaeoloxodon

Right This shows the difference in size between a woolly mammoth and the pygmy version.

Even more dramatic were the tiny creatures that evolved on some islands. Malta, an island in the Mediterranean, was home to an elephant named *Palaeoloxodon* which stood less than a meter (3.2 ft) tall. Such a small size is even more remarkable because only a few miles away on the mainland a similar species of *Palaeoloxodon* grew to a height of 4 m (13 ft). Perhaps the greatest reduction in size was that of the ground sloth on the islands of the Caribbean. On the mainland these creatures were over 4 m (13 ft) long, but on the islands they were about the size of a large rabbit.

The Tar Pits of California

Between about 100,000 and 40,000 years ago large pools of sticky tar bubbled up from the ground near what is now Los Angeles, California. Water lay in thin sheets over this tar, making it look like a cool pond. Many animals that came to drink became trapped in this tar and sucked down into it. As the years passed the tar solidified, preserving the animal bones. Modern scientists have dug up these tar pits. They now know a lot about the animals that lived in

Several types of elephants lived in North America including the mastodon.

Mastodon

20

California thousands of years ago.
   The largest of these animals was
the Imperial mammoth. This
elephant stood over 4 m (13 ft) tall
and had enormous, curved tusks.
And about a meter (3 ft) shorter
was the American **mastodon**.

Saber-tooth cat

Smaller plant-eaters have been found in the tar pits. These include an extinct species of pronghorn antelopes, animals that grazed on the grass of the plains. A type of horse has also been found. However, by far the most common plant-eaters were bison.

A trapped mammoth or bison made a tempting target for **predators** and scavengers alike. But as soon as the animal moved in for the kill, it too became trapped. The most common predators found in the tar pits are saber-tooth cats. These powerful hunters were

Smilodon, a type of saber-tooth cat, hunted and ate large plant-eaters, such as bison and mammoths.

armed with long stabbing teeth
which were very sharp and curved.
The second most common meat-
eater was the dire wolf, a scavenger
which fed on leftovers from a
saber-tooth's meal. Other hunters,
such as mountain lions and foxes,
are found only rarely in the tar pits.
Perhaps these animals were too
alert to get trapped in the sticky tar.

Bison

The Interglacials

On several occasions the glaciers retreated as warm weather returned to the Earth. One of these warm periods, known as **interglacials**, may have lasted as long as 200,000 years. Many of the interglacial periods were much warmer than the climate of today.

As the weather warmed up, plants were able to grow again. The tundra became restricted to the northernmost areas of Asia and North America. Taiga forests disappeared from most of Europe

Below The large and fierce auroch was the ancestor of modern farm cattle.

Auroch

24

Human Hunters

During the Ice Age humans spread throughout the world. These early people were totally dependent on nature for their food. They gathered plants and hunted animals. They used spears and bows and arrows to kill large animals in great numbers. During the Ice Age some species died out completely. It is possible some of the species were hunted to extinction by humans.

Right During interglacials the hippo-potamus lived throughout Europe and much of Asia.

and Asia to be replaced by forests of oak, beech and elm. Animals such as woolly mammoths, musk-oxen and reindeer moved north to follow the new areas of tundra and taiga.

Many areas of Europe and Asia became the home to animals found only in Africa today. A species of straight-tusked elephant, about 4 m (13 ft) tall, moved around in forests and on grasslands. Rivers and pools were home to hippopotamus. These snorting, splashing animals were once common in the Thames River in the south of England. On the banks could be found lions and several species of deer. One of the most impressive animals was the auroch, a huge animal which was the ancestor of modern domestic cattle.

The Americas Meet

For nearly 60 million years before the Ice Age South America was largely cut off from the rest of the world. Mammals on the continent evolved into forms unlike any others on Earth.

Toxodon was a large plant-eating animal which had strong, heavy legs. It was the last in a long line of animals that had gradually increased in size from a creature the size of a large dog, to *Toxodon*, which was as large as a hippopotamus. Even more unusual was a giant armadillo called *Glyptodon*. It was protected by a solid shield of bone over its back and head. The largest were 2.5 m (8 ft) long and ate almost every kind of plant they could reach. Larger than either *Toxodon* or *Glyptodon* was *Megatherium*, which means giant beast. *Megatherium* could rear up on its hind legs to a

Below Toxodon became extinct when the two Americas joined.

Right The Glyptodon was a giant armadillo. Smaller varieties still live in both North and South America. The small hairy armadillo is shown above.

Toxodon

Glyptodon

The two-toed sloth (right) **is a relation of the Megatherium (below).**

Megatherium

height of 6 m (20 ft). This creature was a relative of the sloths which still live in South American trees.

Some unusual meat-eaters also lived in South America. They were all marsupials; that is they raised their young in pouches like kangaroos and koalas in Australia. Perhaps the most powerful of these was *Thylacosmilus*, about 1.4 m (4.5 ft) long. It had long, stabbing teeth like a saber-tooth cat and probably hunted similar prey.

When North America became joined to South America at the start of the Ice Age, the animals of the two continents were able to mix and compete with each other. On the whole the animals of North America were more efficient and took over. Most of the animals of South America died out, but some, such as armadillos, anteaters and opossums, survive to this day.

27

The End of the Ice Age

About 15,000 years ago the most recent glacial period ended. The glaciers and ice sheets retreated northward as the climate became warmer. Slowly the ice and snow melted and new life could return.

As the tundra became warmer stunted willow and birch trees began to grow. These were followed by Scotch pine and fully grown birches. As the years passed the trees became larger and more closely packed until coniferous forest covered the land.

The warm, wet weather changed much of the northern hemisphere. Dense forests of **deciduous** trees became common. Oaks, elms, lindens and other trees grew and spread to become forests. Boars, bison, aurochs, wolves and bears began to live in these forests.

Right A shepherd grazes his sheep.

Humans appeared in great numbers as the ice retreated. Instead of simply hunting animals and gathering plants, these people were farmers. They cleared forests to use the soil to grow food crops. Wild animals were wiped out as domestic cattle, pigs and sheep were introduced. Humans were introducing an entirely artificial enviroment instead of a typical interglacial one.

It is worth remembering, however, that this change may not have been the end of the Ice Age. At the moment we are living in a warm interglacial period. Perhaps in the distant future the ice sheets will begin to advance again. Then it will become impossible for humans to grow crops or live comfortably in most of Europe, Asia and northern North America. It is hard to imagine what life will be like if that happened.

Wild boar

Glossary

Adapt Change to suit different living conditions.

Climate The type of weather typical of a particular region.

Coniferous Bearing cones and needle-shaped leaves. Coniferous trees, such as pine and fir trees, stay green all year round.

Deciduous Shedding leaves every year at the end of the growing season.

Environment The natural surroundings of an area, such as forest, plain or seabed.

Equator The imaginary line that circles the Earth midway between North and South Poles.

Evolved Changed and developed naturally.

Hibernation Spending the winter asleep.

Interglacial A period of time during which glaciers retreated and temperatures rose.

Mammoth An extinct type of elephant.

Mastodon An extinct branch of elephant-like animals.

Migrate To move from one feeding ground to another. Animal migrations usually occur at the same time each year.

Predators Animals that hunt and kill other animals for food.

Prey Animals that are hunted and killed for food.

Species Groups of plants or animals that are members of the same family.

Taiga Forest made up mainly of coniferous trees.

Tundra The open plains in cold regions of the world where no trees or bushes grow and where temperatures rise above freezing for only a few months a year.

Vegetation Plant life.

Books to read

Benton, Michael, **How Dinosaurs Lived.** (Warwick, 1985).

Benton, Michael, **The Story of Life on Earth.** (Franklin Watts, 1986).

Gallant, Roy, **From Living Cells to Dinosaurs.** (Franklin Watts, 1985).

Gamelin, Linda, **Origins of Life.** (Gloucester, 1988).

Jaspersohn, William, **How Life on Earth Began.** (Franklin Watts, 1985).

Lampton, Christopher, **Mass Extinctions: One Theory of Why the Dinosaurs Vanished.** (Franklin Watts, 1986).

Lampton, Christopher, **New Theories on the Dinosaurs.** (Franklin Watts, 1989).

Picture acknowledgments

The photographs in this book were supplied: Bruce Coleman Ltd 7 (Eric Crichton), 27 (Francisco Erize), 26 (Jeff Foott), 5 (Stephen J. Kraseman), 29 (Hans Reinhard), 6 (John Shaw), 25 (Peter Ward); Oxford Scientific Films 12 (Frank Huber), 11 (Tom Ulrich).

Index